2-9-07

To Brendon
Enjoy -

FREE OF ME

Dari

To The New River Valley

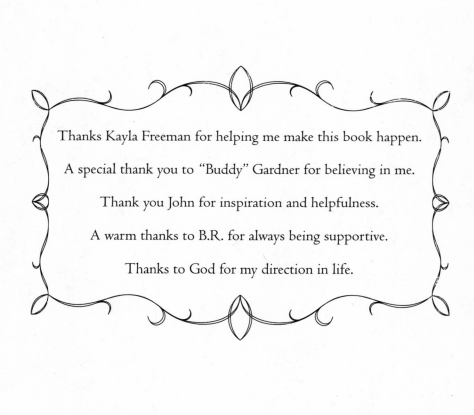

Thanks Kayla Freeman for helping me make this book happen.

A special thank you to "Buddy" Gardner for believing in me.

Thank you John for inspiration and helpfulness.

A warm thanks to B.R. for always being supportive.

Thanks to God for my direction in life.

Table of Contents

I

Free of Me

Years of haunting
Bad memories
Sticking within
A poking to never forget
Recalling of what was
Growing into a new
For the pain
It is fading
Not much returning
This awakening
Has it been
A free of me
Escaping thoughts
Was impossible
Drifting
Feeling of differences
Again it is passing.

Two Rings

A wedding day to come
The moments full of love
This special place
The two will grow
Having happiness
Finding miracles
To be as one
So much to give
For they know
This moment
These days will last
Faith, Love
The tenderness
The day is approaching
Two will be joined
Together
They say forever.

Right There

There she is
A young lady
Having her life ahead
A world big enough
There she is
Sitting here
Waiting for this
Waiting for that
When will it happen
What shall she do
Time is passing
No activity has come
What is the wait
There again she sits
Waiting for the right time.

One More

Here again
It is you and I
Another year to celebrate
A wonderful moment
A joy in your heart
This time it is more
Shall I say
A togetherness
A side by side
You and I
A partnership
Trust and courage
New days
New times
For you and I.

Fitted Not

Your life
Going day by day
No excitement
Sleeping
Wondering
Trying to fit in
Are you cool
No by half
Are you sad
Your eyes show
You live a life
Are you happy
Trying to be
I know how you are
I see
I wish a better life for you
I know.

Don't Do Much

I pray a prayer
May God help you
Possibly you both
No happiness I sense sadness
Praying that you will
Hoping that life
Has a gift to you
You will find it and use it
This is God's creation
Enjoy what is out there
Go live be merry to explore
Time will be there
You are young having no patience
Why must you do all this
That you do not do.

Nothing

Racing head
Wondering mind
Emptiness grows
No wind
Calmness has settled
Still yet
Safety ness has not
Looking
Trying to find
Desperately seeking
Finding what
Laying ahead
Is it comfort
Security
Maybe hope
It is nothing.

Pulling Apart

I wanted to be by your side
Through the years
I see us fading
A friendship to last
Both people
Growing different directions
One seeks another's life
The other seeks a life of unease
Both being there
But are they
Have they grown apart
Not knowing each other
For they have become
Something separate
No alike
Just different.

Choose

His existence is felt
If only you let the self call upon him
Let yourself ask for forgiveness
Reach out with your arms open
To not hesitate
For his love is true
He gave his life for you
So now it is your choice
To either have eternal life
With the Lord, our Father
Or to cast upon this earth
Burn in the lake of fire for all eternity
You can choose.

My Sister

You are a sister
That has come
So far along the way
A sister that has grown
Bloomed into a beautiful lady
A mother of two
Two little precious girls
That reflects upon you.

My sister
A person that sometimes hear the truth
A friend to always be there
Guidance when I need it
And her the same.

Your special
That is why
I am writing this
To let you know
You're my sister
Forever and Always.

Hand in Hand
To my sister.

To Michelle

Why Are They

I am looking around me
Trying to figure out
Why are these people
Like the way
That they are
So sinful
Full of stupidity
Were not suppose to judge
But I wonder
How do they survive
Why were they created
Really God
Was there a purpose
But then there is love
For all of us
When seeing these
Corrupted people
I visualize a nicer place
Praying that they
Those people would just realize
What they really are
Yet still in the back of my head
I ask Lord why.

Small Hearts

A child's heart can reach so many
A child's eye can tell a story
Their faces is loved
A child's heart can be bruised
Bodies can be worn and abused
The minds tormented
A child should be a child
So many crying out
A child's face tells many.

Not Anger

This is not anger this is me
Hoping that you will understand
Expressions may come and go
But wondering if this is meant so
Confused, terrified
Words cannot express
Only holding on to see
If this will last
There are times when disagreements
Will come along
There are those dislikes
But if this is love how come the fights
I can only do so much
Will you help me out
A trust to fulfill
A bond to make
A person to love only me
To love who I am
Mind, body, and soul
Wanting to laugh together
To cry together
To always hold hands
Be there to understand
This is not anger only hope
Hope that one day
You will understand.

Notice What

Closer than realizing
Memories that is not forgotten
A will
A power
Having remorse
A tension
To stare down
Be unknown
Maybe forgotten
Traveling through
Noticing of nothing
A choice
Creations to be seen
A gift of heaven
A wide spread
Happily to be
A closer than
But no less
Than it.

Last Hour

If this is my hour
Then let me be known
Let my soul be free
A way from destruction from sin
Let me just go away
An hour to come no notice
No checking in a freedom a chance
This is to be than let my hour come
Having to go home
Kingdom has come
If this has to be done
Then let it so for my hour has
Will let it be

Amen.

Nature Be

Watching
Letting it sink in
For there is one
A love that has stricken
Watching
Given life to me
A power to be set free
A peace that comes
Watching
For this love
This pleasure
Goes on day to day
Seeing and believing
Watching
Nothing so beautiful
Sitting and listening
Watching
Seeing all that is
Around Nature.

It Will Come

One day
It will come
A chance to see
To show or be
A moment to
No sadness
Waiting for it
When the days increase
Time moves so does it
There someday it will
Having to appear
Your chance your time
One day.

Standing Tall

Standing tall
Giving orders
No smile to make
Only wanting work to be done
Confusion you give
No patience
No wasting the time
Slapping the hand
Quantity comes first
You have authority
Looking down upon others
Wanting them to fear
I ask why
No friends to make
How could it be
You have no control
Losing the mind
Unstable you are
Something has been
There before
A state of mind
Wondering if its right
There before
Are you
Just standing tall.

Tour

Poorness
Visitor come
Tourist pays
Education is made
Visiting beautiful sites
Seeing many discoveries
There sits
On the side of the road
Poorness grows
Attractions around
Friendly smiles
Glad to see
People from all around
Some sadness
They go on
Living their lives
We come down
Vacation is made
Their lives stay
Paradise
Then again
There is poorness.

Warm Smile

Smiling with sunshine
Breathing fresh air
Remembering times
My eyes open the heart growing
Being and feeling there you are
Arms wide enough
No tears no shame
Simple gesture
Warm and tender
Smiling with sunshine.

MX

There it was
Here we were
Can cun
This is Mexico
People lots of them
From England
Canada to Brazil
Temperatures hot
The water unbelievable
Beauty all around
White sands
Palm trees
Coconut
So much more
Tours daily
Downtown crazy
Play a del Carmen
Cozumel what a ball
Chichen Itza worth seeing
There it was
We were there
Can cun.

Intermix

Is this a between
A world of angels
Demons and half breeds
Living among us in this world
Are those watching and waiting striking out
Can we see a world of such sin
Not knowing what real Hell is like
Torture to be
There is a place of peace
Somewhere there is ease.

Dolphin Discovery

The Royal Swim
Some training
Touches and feels
Creatures were kind
Dolphins were real
Swimming
Feeling free
Lifting of the feet
Flying high
Gliding
Smacking the water
Flippers wave
Whispers were made
Sounds heard
Pictures taken
Video was there
Excitement took place
Time flew
Moments were gone
Finishes were done.

Joy to Be

Fullness tightness occurs
Mind wondering thinking possibly
Confused yet so there
Heartache breathless
Racing for truth
Patience everlasting
To be so
A love that grows
Giving thanks
A true blessing happiness.

Baby Shower

Gifts around
Lots of smiles
Presents to open
Games to play
Much of the food
In a couple of weeks
This tiny precious
Will come into a world
To meet
A mothers face
Will be for all
To come and see
A warmth
A love like no other
Bonding
A safe place
Comfort to feel
A freshness
A feel
In a couple of weeks
You will be
A mother of joy.

Hurry Life

We all grow up in a hurry
If it was not the war
There was the farm work
If not that pressure of education
Maybe even marriage
Having children
Children being abused
Making childhood disappear
We all grow up in a hurry.

Sitting Beside

Falling in love again
Those days of relaxing
Enjoying the site
Sitting on the beach
Watching the waves
Holding hands
Soaking up the sun
Falling in love again
Remembering when
Making your eyes bright
Laughter to hear
Being silly
Living the dream
Making life happen
Driving long hours
Finding discoveries
With you
These are made possible
Falling in love again
Over again.

Grandma's Love

A house that is open
Grandma's are special
They are there for you
They love taking in what some may not
Hugs and kisses
Smiles that is all around
Smelling the good cooking
A fullness that lasts
Grandma's are special
For they give so much and love.

Discovering

Discoveries
Places to visit
To make people see
Hear the voices
Smells of different
Sights to see
Beauty known
Relax
Enjoy the moments
Time healed
Escaping
Paradise
Waiting for joy
There is excitement
Sun blistering
Soaking it within
Saltiness
Taste
There are discoveries
Places to visit
I have seen.

At the Beach

Crashing of the waves
The smell of salt
The taste of easiness
Looking out
Into the distance
Seeing peace
Reaching to it
Mind being
To stare within
Beauty stays
A sound worth hearing
A love to hang onto
Feet getting wet
Feeling the crunchy sand
Seeing the white torn
Mystery as it is
Wonders to be
Feeling the power
Discovering
Seeing and feeling
Smelling at the beach.

A Sight

As your struggling
In the wind
The umbrella
Which has turned inside out
With the rain pouring in
The dog tugging wildly
The leash stretching
The Foodlion bag
Has just torn
Spilled all the goods
Onto the ground
All this was such a sight
So you just took
A deep breath in
And smiled with a laugh
As the rain came.

Unexplained

He spends hours
Many hours
Building a project
For the one he loves
Finally finished
Gives it to her and she said
"This is all you have for me"
He dropped his mouth
And could not explain
He spent time after time
And that is all she can say
He told her that
It was from his heart
After that she said
"Oh, well since you put it that way"
And she smiled.

For You Today

The gigantic ocean
Took my breath away
As I stepped
Right up to it
And said
Hello there
How are you today
It splashed at me
Waved right back
And I knew
It wanted to play
Hopping right in
Not taking to long
Pushing me under
No time at all
The gigantic ocean
Took my breath away.

Horse Ride

Sitting there talking
I seen her come out
The woods being still
As the horse picks up speed
Going faster and faster
All of a sudden
She is falling
With her head
Smacking the ground
I ran fast then faster
To see her laying there
Praying is all
What has happened.

To Spread

Take care of them
Treat them right
For they are so young
And learning off of you
Their minds still developing
Should not have the fear
Respect them
For they will respect you
As just the same
Be their guides
Be their friends
A mother
They are your children
They love
So they should be loved
Spread and share.

If No Tomorrow

If the tomorrow never comes
I just wanted you to know
The times spent
Was so much fun

If I don't get to see the next day
I want you to know
That you and I
Were really meant to be

You mean so much to me
You really do
You are the angel always
My angel looking after me.

Thinking Of You

Oh brother
For I think about you
Which you don't know
Us growing up
Having our fights
Now you're gone
Gone away
Wondering how you
Are doing this day
And how things
Are going in your life
How is your way
Is it the way you wanted
Your plans
Your goals
Did they come true
Was it what you thought
It to be
Do you like it so
Oh brother
For I am thinking
Wondering about you.

Gather Your Seeds

Gather your seeds
Little feathered friends
All scattered out
Hunting for food
As one finds the other grabs
Wanting to take
Eat little guys
Feathered friends
There is not much
Not much this time of year.

3 Rose Play

Watching Eyes
Drawn only towards
To her the one
That is the play
The play
Feeling the emotions
The sadness
The fear
Depression
For she does
So good
Wanting to bring tears
Telling us about life
Going by before eyes
Some are here
Some asleep
Not knowing what is
Three Roses
Two Rose
One Rose.

The Flow

Hands together
Eyes meeting
Us softly gliding
Across the dance floor
The music playing
No other feeling around
Grinning and laughing
Wanting to have this dance to last
The whole night
With a sweet kiss
Setting the romance
This flow.

No Keeps

Her life is like
An open book
For all to see
Seeing upon
Her face
In her lonely eyes
Many years
Passing
By and by
What does she have
Having to show
Only nothing
For she thinks
She does try
So hard
But do they
Take away
Giving up
Hope
Giving it up
She getting
Very weak
Weaker each day.

What Is Inside

Looking around
I see many
Many things
When I see
A particular
Place or person
That interests me
I write it down
Upon the paper
For all to someday
One day read
Expressing it
Into another form
A form of poetry
My head
Getting full of ideas
Ideas of everything
Wanting to help
Helping in many ways
I cannot become
Those many things
For that would take
Years and years
So I'm writing
Writing and giving
A chance to read
To read
To gather
What lies inside.

Best Friend

Who could be
That true friend
The best friend
Someone to be
There through
It all
To love
When things begin
To fall
To guide
To show
To help
To cry
Telling you no lies
Speaking their mind
No truth hidden
When you find
The true friend
That is there
Keep them close
By hanging on
Keep them for life
For they are
A friend
A true friend.

Stay With

Please
Please
Do not die
On me
I want you
To be with me
Here
Here in this life
Do not go
I need for you
To stay
I love you
So much
Does that count
I will hold on
If you will
Please
Please
Stick with me
You can do it
I know you can
You are strong
So young
It will not happen
It will not
No not this
Not now
Stay with me
Please!

Not Believing

This is not
Happening
You were suppose
To get old
Get gray
Helping me out
When I needed
Your guidance
No one was there
I will not
I cannot
Believe this now
This is too much
Too much pain
My heart
My heart is hurting
Pounding so hard
Why did you go
Leaving me so
I am alone
This pain
The pain will last
Building up inside
I know.

The Approach

Coming back
From lunch
Going through
The parking lot
When I seen
An older guy
Raising his hand
Down then up again
Slowly kept going
I thought maybe
Something was wrong
I pulled to the side
Asking him
What is wrong
He smiled
Then he gave a reply
I have seen you around
Haven't I
I was wondering
He said
If you would like
I will sell you this
To get high
Stunned I was
Standing there
Thinking
What in the world
This man
I do not know
Asking just anybody
I said no thanks
Turning away
Thinking this
Could have been
A small child
He came to ask.

Your Child

The little children
Why cause them
To suffer
Suffering by the neglect
Not wanting any
Although you have them
No love
Only pain
Cause you hate
Not being a family
But may be
There is afraid
Running around
After hours
Them following
You didn't leave
Them behind
Being so fragile
They are so tired
Can you not see
There is hurt
In their eyes
Falling down
Them being so irritated
And you wonder why
Take a good look at them
They are hurting inside.

To Build

Lets get together
Get together
And have some fun
Putting everything behind
To only have some fun
Lets get a way
Get a way from this place
To full fill our dreams
With only
You and me
To build the dream house
To live the nice life
For the sun will shine
You will bring
The glow into my eyes
Lets build.

Sets Low

The sky has many
Many colors
As the sun
Sets low
Reminding me
Of a rainbow
How nice it goes
Like a beautiful
Rainbow
Reminds me of
A skittle
With their
Also so many colors
As the sun sets low
It has so many
Many colors.

That Day Of Goodbye

He thought
About her
Missed her so
Wanted to call out
To tell her
How he really
Does feel
That he cares
Somehow
He did not
Did not speak
Watched her go
Waved goodbye
She waving back
Tears in her eyes
Not knowing
What she wanted
Because he never
Knew she was there
Now she is gone
He realizing
Was this a mistake
Such a mistake
It is too late
She has gone.

Consistency

What you model
Is what they learn
You try to tell them
What is wrong
And what is right
They see you if you smoke
Or use bad language
Still yet you say its bad
You know to say it
You do not know
How to do it
The children reflect
What they see
You cannot teach
If your not
Willing to go along
You have to show
Be an example
A good example
And they will
Will follow along.

Go Away

Every time I close my eyes
The dreams haunt me scaring me
Like the past that never dies
In reality I go on with my life
But my dreams
They keep me under control
Like a prisoner
A prisoner to never escape
If only my dreams
Those bad memories
Would just go away.

Crawlers

Running so fast
So hard
But it seemed as though
My feet were not moving
Out of breath
Wanted to escape
How do I
Nothing I could do
Just to run
To try to run
Their behind me
Following me
Every step that I make
Their legs
Seemed long
Enough then
They spread
This is only a dream
I know it is
Why can't I awake
For the spider
They getting closer
Closer
And closer.

To Learn

Why do people question
Is there a God
Just because
You cannot see Him
Some people practice magic
And you believe it
Why not God
Everybody has their religions
Some have none at all
The confused ones
Trying to search
But for what
Do people have a chance
A chance to learn
Or may it be to late
Late to learn about God.

Down the Road

Taking a long walk
To ease my mind
On the side of the road
Sits a pile of snow
In the creek just below
The ice is building upon
Leaving only a path
A tiny path
For the water to flow
All you can see is a layer of ice
Trying to squeeze through below
Walking down this street
On a calm day
Then something comes
Over me in my mind
But I just cannot say.

To Appreciate

As we go down the streets
Looking nice and pretty
With the clothes on our backs
And the shoestring tied neat
Do we every stop to think
About the others, the people
If they ever have anything to eat
When we hug or kiss our partner
Or our family
Do we appreciate
That we are loved
There is so much out there
That we have and use
Yet we do not stop to think
How grateful we are
Most people cannot even
Pick up a book or a paper
Or a poem to read
Take a minute
Do you realize
You have so much
That millions of others
Wished they had.

One Smile

When you smile
There is much light shown
You brighten my place
With just one smile
When you are around
You always seem
To have that smile
That one smile.

Focus Please

When I talk
Do you listen
When I say something
Do you focus on only me
How many times
Do I have to repeat
Do I have your attention
What about when you speak
Do I act the same way
I am able to listen
To give you my full attention
When I speak
Do you even listen.

Sleep Time

Go to sleep
Little brother
For I am by your side
No harm
Will come your way
I promise little one
For I will protect you
All the way
Go to sleep
Little brother
Me and the Angel
Will pray
Close your eyes
Close your eyes
For I will see you
In the morning
My little one
For now it is
Sleep time.

Hidden Inside

A young girl running
Trying to run away
From what
From all this pain

A young lady
Still running
Trying to run away
From what
What is hidden inside
Her today

When she closes her eyes
Still the same thing
She wants to scream out
But the fear she has
She might get the blame

Only wanting the pain
This pain to go away
For someone to take her
Far, far away.

Little One

A curious boy
Wondering what I am doing
Asking many questions
Some I can explain
A young face
So fragile and so pale
Wondering what I can tell
His eyelashes so long
The eyes being so tired
I wonder what he knows or hides
Having only the strength to go on
I do and care for him
For he is so very tiny
All I can do and really do
Is try to protect him
A curious boy
A very little boy.

The Moment

Live every second
As it would be your last
Seize every moment
That you have
The past is gone and yet
We are not promised
For the future
We only have the moment
This moment
We need to live it
Live it and forget about the past
But do not go to far
Into the future
Live today
Only this moment.

Who Cares

The work stinks
So why are you still there
Getting reports written
On you
When you're just trying
To prove
Every one is
Being unfair
But they say
That's life
Who wants to care
That is the problem here
No one wants
To get involved
So they keep their heads down
Acting like a puppet
Floating in the air
Work does stink
But you try to make it a team
Like they say
Who cares.

All The Way

Come now come
You don't have to be afraid
Come now come
I will give no harm
But to show you the way
The journey is long
And I am here to keep your chin up
So we must go on
You and I all the way.

Pounding

My eyes are watching
My mind is listening
And my thoughts
They do not want to end

My heart pounds
When you are around
And my hands
They want to touch

When your out of my sight
I wonder when
When I'll get to see you again

I miss you so
I want you to know
And I hope you do see
That I am not fake

That I love you
And I want to stay.

Seeds Begin

There within a miracle is about to happen
The flow of genetics
The gathering of the seeds
A new life to form
Starting a success
A sense of being only within
That miracle will begin.

Feels Like

Do those dreams
Feel real
Tensed, emotional
And feeling great
Your body twists
Tightens
Then feeling loose
The dreams
Can they hurt
Haunt and scare
Smashing the heart into
What about the dreams
Those dreams.

The Island

The ocean on one side
The sound on the other
Your going straight forwards
With not much around
The sand piled high
The other side flat
Not seeing it in person
Can you visualize it
Well it may bring a wonder
Being there it is different
So peacefully so nice
Makes you want to only stay
This island.

The Goal

If you think you are afraid
Of what is around
Then it will haunt you
If you want to succeed
But have doubts
Then you probably will not
If you think you cannot win
Then you will lose
There is much out there
And it is all in the state of mind
If you think you can
Then you can
You have to think about
The above
And not the below
Then you will become
A stronger person inside
You will
You will accomplish your goals.

Storm

Storms arising
Viewing the strikes
Across the blue sea
Darkness grows
Wind smears
Sand blown
The smell of fresh rain
Touch of drops
Against the skin
Water rises
Puddles are made
For the storm begins.

No Care No Share

Someone gives so much
So much love
So much caring
And is willing to share
Giving so much to others
That they don't see
That person is there
Taking what they can get
And never no returns
Although that person
Asks for nothing
But I know their only
Wanting to at least have a smile
Or a thank you would be fine
Doesn't anybody take the time
To stop and say hey
What are we thinking
It is our turn
Our turn to return the favor
The love and the caring
To have even the sharing.

The Day

That day took her life
The memories of love
Memories of warmth
No movement to make
Numbness stays
A split second all hopes are gone
Depressed
Why me the thoughts remained
An innocent drive the other strikes
Realization awakes
That day.

Through the Door

Why do you sneak
Within my door
Never knocking
Coming straight in
Without a trace
No footsteps to make
Usually I do get scared
Only because someday
It could be another
At my door
Coming in without the steps
Sneaking upon me
Without having a familiar face
Understand now
Please don't come through
My door
Acting as if you
Get thrills
Off seeing the expressions upon
See here
NO MORE.

Hurts Inside

Why do you say
Her name more than you do mine
You may not know
But it does hurt me so
Joking or playing around
It is no fun
No game to me
When you are near
Your eyes go past mine
To look upon hers
Why do you do that
Don't you know
That it hurts me inside
Can't you see that
That pain laying in my eyes
I ask you why.

No Awake

Rush upon
Let the midnight dreams come
Come to fear
Screaming sounds
The cries getting loud
Rush upon
Like the burning sun
How many people are getting hurt
Upon those hills
The dreams never ending
For you will never see the awake
Faces the faces
Their horrible
And the bleeding inside
The pain is pounding
Never to see the awake.

Wanting Someone

I want to explore my dreams
To make them happen
For them to all come true
I want someone to love me
With all the love they have
Never giving up on me
Just holding each others hand
Through the falls
Guiding one another
Through this life
Expecting the rights and wrongs
I am wanting so much more
But can only take one step
One step forward
Is there someone out there
Out there that can love me
For who I am
Is there someone out there
That would share
To explore my dreams
With me.

To Speak Up

I know I should speak up
But my mouth tends to not open
Remembering of only the past
That little girl again
All alone
Afraid to say no
What is the matter with me
My response is afraid
I am afraid
Of what they might do
People may laugh
What will they say
But this is wrong
Their men
And I must have this to stop
I am not that little girl
I have rights
My own mind
I will take a step forward
For once I will not hide
I will speak up
For this I say is my life.

Choices

The choices that we make
Affects us everyday
There are those choices
Hard choices easy choices
What is the right choice
Every time we awake right then
Like what shall we do today
If it wasn't for one choice
We may not have been here
Choices its what makes the day.

Riding

The wind
The fresh air

Running about 60
Legs relaxed

You're there

The motor beneath
Arms stretched

Running along
Smooth then lean
Leaning into the curves

You're there

Beneath is asphalt
Seeing the clear blue sky

The weather perfect
Smelling the fresh air

You are so very there.

Together

Life is sweeter
More understanding
With the both of us
Precious times to look forward
Past adventures we had
This relationship will grow
Full of trust, surprises and love
When there is a sad face
I offer you a smile
To accept gladness
Not sadness
This life will offer much
With the both of us
We can pull through
What God has given us
To be together
With our faith
We can walk hand in hand.

How Can You Recall

A life without nothing
There is so much
Yet I hear I want more
A world obsessed
Wanting when they have
Greedy, hungry for being
The eyes are full
Glorious, fame then honor
But what is all of this
Will it matter in the next life
Should a person have it all
Why for this world will pass
A wonderful place is to come
For only the saved.

Stand Together

There is a state
There is many states
There is a government
There are laws
How does one run as government
Or President
And their heart is not clean
How could a person rule
Over many
But does not know God
"Justice For All"
Then they take away
The right to speak of God
What is wrong
What is right
Is the constitution
Really being followed
Making up as they go along
How can a person say
I follow Christ
But their life shows different
This nation our nation
We need to stand up
For what is right.

Repeating Steps

I usually see you cleaning
Everyday back and forth
The same old pace
When someone
Walks in the path
You repeat yourself
Continuing to go back
Clean, clean
That is your objective
Your job
Somehow today
I had to help
Even though
I shouldn't have
It was your job
But you were running behind
And I know
How time flies
I had to lend you a hand
For you were repeating
Repeating your steps.

V

Thinking Back

There she was
Thinking back upon
Those memories
While the wind softly blowing
Blowing through her dark hair
The sun beaming onto her soft shiny
Dark lips
The summer days that she had
Was very merry
Having so much fun
Smiling and how her green eyes
Do brighten
She is enjoying life
And looks around
Observing all she can.

Too High

There are the taxes
Taxes of all kind
There are the bills
Bills of all sorts
The gas is high
And may go even higher
The jobs are low
People getting laid off
And still yet
They expect us to pay
Pay for what
Their expenses
The doings of their own
Life is high
Life is too high.

Earnhardt

That Sunday evening
When the race was going
Still going
Accidents happening
Crashing going
Still, everyone was o.k.
Then it hits
The last lap
Faces went down
The crowd
They were in shock
When they heard
Earnhardt is hurt
Then there were frowns
He was the man in racing
With a strong and heard name
That Sunday at 49 years old
People had hopes
He went against that wall
The faces all the faces had fear
Dale Earnhardt was gone.

Order

Order, order
Will the first witness please stand
Order, order
For I will not say again
This is a courtroom
My courtroom have respect
For me and the person whom to stand
Everyone is innocent until proven guilty
Don't you know
So put down those hands
Order, order.

Half My Day

Hello welcome to Wal-Mart
No that is not my line
I usual sit or stand
Watching and waiting
Then people come by
They go to work saying
How are you or
How are you doing today
Then I have to say
Fine, o.k. or usually all right
About a hundred times
I get asked the same question
Then going by me they say
Have a good day or
Have a good one
Yeah right.

One Day

She cannot go without one day
One day without anyone
Anyone bothering her
Going to school coming home
The roommates bug her
Making those comments
She just wants to hear a sweet remark
Not a flick you out the door
At work she feels the eyes upon
As some question
What did you wear last night
If there was just one day
One day to go to school come home
Go to work without anyone
Anyone messing in her place
Her space for just one day.

Too Busy

Busy busy
Everyone is too busy
To stop and look at nature
To smell the trees and leaves
The flowers are beautiful
Hearing the birds sing
To actually enjoy
A piece of chocolate
Or any kind of food
Putting the piece into your mouth
To feel the texture
The sweetness melt
Everyone is so busy.

To Relax

Relax go ahead
And just relax
Think of nothing
Only the happiness
Maybe about a place
A place that you wish could last
Go ahead and feel the warmth
The sun upon
As you walk along
Taking deep breaths in then out
The thoughts are clear
Wanting to assuage all
Thats what seems to be pain
Relax just relax.

The Problem

To whom it may concern
You know I have
This problem
Or could it be you
Are the problem
You make me feel
As if I am the problem
To whom it may concern
Maybe I am right
Or is it that you are right
The problem is simple
The problem is
Definitely you.

Outer Space

I am here but usually I feel
As if I am not here
My mind wondering
The thoughts flying
And I am here
Trying to focus
Trying to give answers
To what I don't know myself
From experience that is
I am here and I can listen
But usually I feel
As if I am somewhere.

Much To Come

Two people meet
Make love in about a month
That month goes by
Now talking about marriage
Having one kid
But not the father
They believe they want to go on
Both so young
Still having much to come
Still yet they are going to be wed
Two people meet
Both has much to come.

Your Visions

Are you afraid
Afraid of what
Your thoughts
The visions
When you dream
Do they haunt you
Why would they
Do you or they
Go the other way
Putting them behind
Only behind
You know
Not letting them out
Makes things worse
Are you afraid
Afraid of what
What the people
May say.

Someday

She is washing away
Washing away in those tears
Drifting just drifting
Away in those tears
Someday the sun will shine
Shine upon her
Giving a smile
To dry those tears
Those lonely tears
Someday.

Asleep

She knew no harm
Would come her way
Not while they were there
They loved her
So like all parents do
They have a child
But something happened
For they did not see
Its not that they
Did not care
It wasn't that
For they were
Merely asleep
The touches
The feels
Were happening
She never cried
Only drifting away to
Another place
Making her feel safe
She did not know
Was this suppose to be.

Young Love

Just one thing
Why get married
At such an early age
Because you say you are in love
Well then if you are so in love
Why don't you just wait
Wait for that special moment
That special time in place
Not to hurry
Getting married
Having kids
They can wait
They'll be there
Think what is next
After you've done that
What is next.

Racing By

Racing by me so fast
In a hurry with your feet
Heading out the door
Slamming it behind
Then as you go right out
You hit the pavement
And begin to roll
As I see you come back
You seem o.k.
Not even a scratch
Racing by
Racing on back.

Cape Hatter's Light

As approaching
The light was shining
The breeze flowing
The night air being just right
Upon the sidewalk
We stand looking up
There it was standing so tall
We moved in closer
Feeling of the sand beneath
As we watched
Taking every second in
Every minute within us
For it was so nice
Enjoying this calmness
Peaceful night
Looking at this light.

Believe

Look up and believe
For He died
For you and me
On that cross
Then He arose
He wants us to know
To believe
Walk thy path
You shall see
For He loves you so
Yes He does
You and me.

Outer Banks

Upon the ferry
Going out to what seems
Like nowhere
Only the ocean that surrounds
Further and further away
No land in sight
For that you could not see
Until you reached
Reaching the other side
The waves were calm
As we rode along
Coming up after
It took awhile
Is the land ahead
The island that we finally reached
The part of destination
The Outer Banks.

The Coldness

Such coldness is in the air
As the soft snow comes
Comes pouring down
The wind slapping the faces
While the little noses are red
The howling of the wind
You try to stay inside
Getting warm
Getting very warm
But there is no hot chocolate
There is such coldness around
This March day
Wanting to see the sunshine
To warm the faces
Such coldness on this day.

Dreamland

Come little one
Come big ones
I can show you the way
From far above
Into another land
Come to me and I will show
Showing you all your dreams
For you will surely see
A place you will play
Play all day
Without having any shame
Come far I can show you that way
For is called Dreamland.

Secrets

He has secrets
She has secrets
What are secrets
They are unsaid words
He loves one
Then loves another
He cannot tell one
But tells the other
Secrets are unsaid
But take more than
One to make secrets
She is a one man woman
Then comes another
She loves one
Then loves the other
He and she want to love another
But there are secrets
Unsaid words.

-Anonymously

Homeless

There was no bed
For me to lay
My head on at night
No bathroom
For us to wash our feet
There was no water
In that dark and gloomy place
Only a blue
Rubbermaid container
Big enough
To only wash off our face
The water
There was none
Going to the gas stations
To get some
My hope
It was fading
Homeless
For the first time
I now realize
What others go through everyday
Without a bed
To lay upon at nights
No comfort
Feeling emptiness
A filth that will not
Come off.

Good Morning

I awake and can hear
The sound that you make
Smelling the breakfast
That you are so kind to cook
As I rise with a wide smile
Upon my face
I then look
Within myself
And can see
That we have become
So much more
Than the beginning
Our love for each other
Growing more and more
Each and everyday
I realized you have given me
So much and so many smiles
You slowly came into the room
Eyes smiling at me
You so softly spoke
"Good morning."

Caffeine

No caffeine
No caffeine
What do you mean no caffeine
Could this only be a dream
Without the caffeine
But how is this
Why does this have to be without
The oh dear my caffeine
I'm missing you
Do you miss me?
Oh my, no caffeine.

Umm, Umm

That chocolate
That chocolate pie
Is winking at me
Boy is it catching my eye
The pie it is
It's calling my name
Oh that chocolate pie
How do I hesitate
Maybe just a little piece
It wouldn't hurt
No, just a tiny piece
I really cannot wait
Umm, Umm
So delicious
I can feel it inside
So tasty
Just one more
One more piece
Of that so rich
Tasty chocolate pie
Umm, Umm

To Be A Giver

To stand alone
You are the giver
With a strong heart
And a lot of patience
If you meet the taker
And you are the giver
Then you will never have anything to complete
The taker will always take
Leaving you alone to make it incomplete
One must meet another giver
So both can give
And not always take.

What Shall I Do

How do I become
How do explain this pain
I hold inside
Yes it has been awhile
Very sad
But I have no idea
Where to begin
These dreams
Never go away
Leaving me confused
My own thoughts
I cannot control
My dreams seems to bleed.

Pathways

Which path do you follow
The path that makes you insane
Which is the pathway to hell
With no desire
But only greed and hate
A path that you live everyday
Blaming something
And someone else
Not wanting to admit
That you were wrong
That you do make mistakes
Tell me, which path
Do you choose
Which pathway do you follow
A path to success
To love and cherish
A love greater than you have ever met
To dream, to fulfill
To maybe even wish upon that very star
Or your same ways the not wanting.

To Whom

I know I need to forget about you
But someone I cannot
Every since we met that day
My life seemed to changed
And my dreams became lighter
Wondering if there could have been a chance
Even a day for us to start a new life
What time we shared
Brought on the happy tears
Now I am just sitting back
Thinking and hoping
Of what is my next goal or plan
Having to force myself to go on
Knowing that you are away
Out there
And just maybe
Maybe I might get to see you some day.

No Return

Having this dark side
Not wanting to
Something keeps these dreams alive
For they are real
Happening every day
Creeping upon
Without a trace
Breathing silently
For there is no face
Crossing from one side to the other
But the mind wonders
Feeling of losing
The body lifts
The soul is lost
Nothing returns.

The Last

Before my last breath
I want to confess
Before my last breath
I have to admit
I have always loved you
From the minute you stepped in
My whole world
My life has changed
Things have flown
So quickly this past year
I have never had the chance
To share my whole heart
With you, my sweet dear
When I am gone
I will look after the one
That I love from above
And want to always
See that smiling face
That glow
But the touch, it will have to wait
You're probably wishing
That you, yourself
Should of told me the same
Those words I love you
Please is it o.k.
I have always known
From the look in your eyes
The pounding of your heart
When it beats so hard
Before my last breath
Let me see that smile
That beautiful smile
Upon your face
So when I close my eyes
I will have just the same.

Two Days

Tortured and beaten
Nothing for that one person to say
Hitting on the head
The blood saturating into the hair
No one around to protect
For no one to hear the sounds
Wanted only to die
To have no more of this
Did not care to go on
Which never came
From the killers
Knew and still gave all the pain
Stone Wall
Was it the battle
That brought this play
The telling of the war
The acting of the truth
Songs were played
Hearts were touched
But coldness grew
For the thoughts
Were only to kill
The battle began
Many, many were butchered
Shot, some raped, and buried with no name
A play of sadness, confusion
Yet all this was once real
Is it a shame.

Some Party

Some party they say
What a party
Never seen anything like it
As the owner brings out the chain saw
Cutting two holes
Then later everyone gathers
To see the skull slide
Into the house
A finished project
A weird project
Taking pictures being amazed
For the house
Is it becoming a boat house
This party of wonders.

To Take Me Out

You brought me into this world
And I know you can take me out
Looking up to you
Trying to respect you
Never to talk back
Hurting me and slapping me
Cutting me but I still
I loved you for that
Not understanding
Why this has to be
But this was our life
You wanted it to be this way
You choked me but never again
Was you afraid
What was going through mind
For I was afraid
You brought me into this world
And I know you can take me out.

Someone There

Needing someone to set sail
You were there
To both catch the breeze
Hearing the splash of the waves
Seeing the sun sparkle
Upon the blue ocean
Wanting that special time to escape
To head for paradise
You were there
Walking along the golden beach
I found treasure
A chest full of love
Someone to share it with
By my side you were there.

Ride Wet

Riding on
Getting caught
By the heavy rain
Shoes drenched
Socks not getting over
For the dryness will come later
Squeakiness as they walk
The helmet fogged
No helping out
For the shield if opened
Rain pours in
Gladly finding my face
The chain needs oiled
For this down pour
An unexpected time
Not prepared for it at all
Riding along getting wet
Yet smiling and enjoying.

Kawasaki

Pushing the start button
The sound fires
There chrome
Stares at you
Clean polished
And ready
This Vulcan 800
The classic kind
Nice fenders
Again it is ready
Swinging the leg over
Taking a seat
Comfortable
The hands in place
Shift in first
Throttle
Taking off so sweet
Smooth
No vibration
Speeds in no time
This is a bike
My kind of bike
Catch me.

Same Room

The girl in the same room
Turns to look
What she does not know
Is that he catches her eye
The man in the same room
Looks over his shoulder
What he happens to see
Is a woman of mystery
There is a move
Both chat
Finding friends
What becomes of two
No knowing of each other
Listening all night
Laughing
In the same room
There was a connection
So much attraction
In the end
They go their separate ways
In the same room.

A New Love

Funny what is that
I hear it
But what is not funny
Is spending eternity
In that lake of fire
All around me
I smell burned skin
For the lust
The cheating
I hear the abuse
A world so beautiful
Taken advantage of by sin
What is there
Is it funny
I once was there
Thinking it will never change
Going on being that sinner
But I had to change
Life is shown differently
Peace came over
Calm to feel
To see this new love
To feel the new love.

Beach House

A dream to live
Feeling the salty breeze
The warmth of the sand
A beautiful house
Relaxing
Everyday a vacation
Walking along the ocean
Seeing many footprints
Upon that golden beach
The crash of the waves
Seagulls flying
Tasting the crisp air
Time spent
Upon the deck
Looking out
The endless blue
Seeing beyond beauty
Miles of the sea
An endless time
The perfect sun
Again a dream to live
Here in this
Beach House.

The Other Side

A point of view
From the other side
Seeing what lies
In front of a person
So sweet and nice
Yet is not there
A love that was strong
A beginning that seemed forever
What is it what has changed
A feeling of lost
Friendship stays
What else is there
Memories that were made
Maybe it's the other
Sometimes wondering
If the connection has cut off
A touch would be nice
Kind gestures
Even a flirtatious wink
Sweetness of a laugh
To look at me
Being from the other side
Wondering and thinking
What will the future be
How will it end
Possibilities
Hopes and dreams to be not afraid
A cuddle of a hug
This affection means a lot
Others would stray
Deciding if I should stay
To live a lifetime of friends
Brings loneliness in every way
Make a connection
A love to last
From the other side.

Room

The room was chilled
Tension and stares
Time was stopped
Trying to make a few jokes
The judge in the next room
What was going on
How would things go
The case only
Was it enough
Who would break down
What will fall
There it comes
Being a supporter
Observing
Seeing and hearing
The room was cold
Frozen into time
The final came
The thumbs were up.

New World

A world has awaken
Something arising never before
Thought about a new world
Yet people blind to see
A power beyond control
Enemy taking over
What will happen
What to become
Destruction as it will
Listening viewing
Time has its play
A new world has it begun.

There That feeling

That feeling is back
There chewing its way
Attacking what is left
This loneliness
Why does it linger
How to escape
This evil that haunts
Giving me many thoughts
Decisions to be made
Here grinding
Touching the only
Things that I have
To be strong
Yell out and scream
Give this loneliness away
No more
For I get weak
Yet I stand tall
Wiping it off
Flinging it into a direction
That it does not want to be
That feeling.

Stop Hungry

It saddens me to see
This hungry
A world full of dreams
So many are in need
Other countries are desperate
Poor, fragile and dieing
Here before us
Is happening the same
Our eyes go beyond not believing
There is no time to help out
Walk on by to not see
What is this selfishness
Overwhelming of hungry waits
The little feet begs mommy
But those cigarettes come first
Pleads to daddy but drugs over rule
This hurt brings tears
Does this person whom experiences it
Grow stronger and want to do better
To see the shame
So much kindness to offer
Money to give
To care and lend
But nothing given
A trust gone because of one bad experience
On streets
Signs are held high
In homes abuse is made
Feelings kept inside
One can make a difference
Stop that pain and hungry.

Two-N-One

Wanting to give a gift
That is everlasting
Only have just the two
Vows may be given
Trust is sought
A joining compassion
Giving sweetness
Excitement that both know
A beginning of an awakening
A special that last
Together is forever
Moments will count memories remain
Always giving wanting nothing
But true kindness
Two souls into one body
A commitment cherishing
Enjoying being together
Happiness surrounds
This is what they want a love
Remaining to the end.

Showed Me

Trying to learn a song that I once heard
Touching each note one by one
Then I felt someone near
She softly sat down by my side
And showed me the keys
Moving her precious hands
Her fingers gliding
As I watched I heard
She showed me how to play that song
I once heard before.

Scarlet

Those eyes
That beautiful dress
Was such a match
She never felt no less
When she wore that green dress
And when she smiled
She took your heart away
All the men looked up to her
With no doubt
Wanting to marry
And live a life with her
But the girls were jealous
Did not want her
To fond about
That did not stop her
For she had a cold heart
Only seeking
Making others
To want her
To cause the jealous men
To even love her
There was only one man
That she knew
Thinking she was
In love with him
But he couldn't possibly try her
She gave up her life for him
Though the love
Changed his plans
He was taken
And she never realized
What was lying there
In her face she had it all
And didn't know it
Until it was too late
Butler was gone.

My Sweet Granny

I was only sixteen
The first time I really ever felt
Deserted in this world
Going to see her
What time I could
As she laid upon the bed
The room had always been chilled
As I would slowly walk in
Her eyes sad you could tell
Her skin pale
She skinner then before
I felt so sorry for her
She was the best woman
That I will ever know
And when she died
She took a piece
Of something in us all
That knew her so well
It was a sad end to a full life
A great loss to every one
She had given us so much
So much love so much wisdom
I could not imagine
What I could do without her
My mother was there
At the final end
She knew my granny was gone
Her spirit had flown
Only her little flesh remained
Tired and broken
I can always feel her near
I know she hadn't deserted me
But had left so many words
Feelings and the memories
I shall have
For they will always stay.

What's the Answer

Everything she had
Went through in her life
All she wanted
Was the answers
Why did her mother
Hate her so
Always beating, kicking
And turned her head
The other way
And why did she love
Someone so much
But they gave up
Their life and left her
She was so alone
Which she had been
All her life
People taking
Advantage of her
Knowing she has been
An easy prey
Because she had
A soft heart and cared
Even though
The others didn't
As she grew older
And wiser
She knew much
Of the world around
And knew she had to turn
Her head the other way.

VII

She Survived

Walking towards
The exit
She was finally free
Never felt better
Realizing what
Her whole life was
As she looked up
It hit her
For the first time
Having plenty of it now
And a full life ahead
There was nothing to haunt her
No more answers
To look for
Just to enjoy
And have peace
She was free
Walking into the sunshine
Feeling the warmth
She gave a small laugh
Everything was going
To be fine
But the road
To get there
Was hell for her
And seemed very endless
All through that time
She was a strong woman
She had survived.

- To the abused

Don't Be Shy

Come out sun
Don't you hide
Can't you see
I would like to feel
You so by my side
Come on now
I'm not out here
For nothing
I would like
To get some sun
Upon my face
And if it is not
Too much
I'd like you
To brighten up this day
It is a weekend
And I want it to be
Just right
There you go
Just a little more
Don't be shy now
I'm a little stingy
So I would
Really like to have
It all
If you don't mind.

Further, Further

The walls are drawing closer and closer
And you are in a distant going further and further
The lights getting dimmer
I can hardly make out your face
What is happening
You were so close to me
Now you seem to be fading
Faster and faster away
I'm only screaming out to you
But you seem to not hear
My heart is pounding
More and more
"Please don't leave me here!"

The Watch

The hands are moving
Slowly moving
Each second
Tick tock tick tock
The are slowly moving
If you listen carefully
You can hear it
Tick tick tick
May be if I look away
Time will go a little faster
No…. it has only been
30 seconds
Not much has past
Tick, tick, tick.

To Yell Out

Feeling a little dizzy
But I don't know why
I'm just sitting here
Waiting for the time
To go by
Feels as if things
Around me
Are getting closer
And closer
Smaller then smaller
Trying to rescue me
What is this
My head
Cannot stop
With the thoughts
That I just want
To yell out
Anybody that comes
I believe I will scream
And say "Please let me out!"

Would You!

Can you see me
As I watch you
Would you take my hand
As I take yours
If I kiss upon your lips
Would you kiss me back
When I smell your sweet scent
As you get closer
Can you smell mine as I get nearer
If I slowly say the words
I Love You So
Would you say it back.

Sorrow In the Eyes

From far away
And above
I could see the sorrow
In the eyes
Nothing totally
Different there
But yet not he same
As before
I shall say
While watching
I could feel
A sense of emptiness
Emptiness
That started to surround
As they began
To walk that path
The path of knowing
Knowing too much
Of one another
And a little of
What was around
There was once a passion
A passion that
Had aroused them both
But still there was
The sorrow in the eyes
The pain begins
As I can witness
The love fading
Bleeding out
Their hearts are slowly
Going the opposite way.

When Can I

I am not too old
And not too young
But still yet
I need someone to hold
I would love to see
What lies ahead for me
To grow older
With someone that I care
By my side
To hold and tell me
They do care
And always want
Me to be near
I want to lie down
And go to sleep
With someone by my side
At nights so I can snuggle
To that person loved
To feel their warmth
Even their heart beat
To turn out the lights
And to know
I ask when can I
That I am safe
With the one whom
I dearly love
And to know
That I can keep you.

The Renters Promise

By: B.R. Newman

Rent is due
I know it is true
And maybe a little late
But your money
I do anticipate
The car broke down
So there is no way to town
The kids got the flu
The cat is sick
And the dog is too
If not for this misfortune
I would have
The money from you
In the end
It will not fail
She tells me
The check is
Already in the mail.

Not You

You judge me for who I am
What I do and say
You dislike my looks
My actions are no good
Why does it have to be this way
Everything I am you make a remark
Must I say does it have to be this way
Why this action
This frown those words
For it all hurts
I am me
I am not you.

To a New Day

Every day has its own little way
Every hour has its minutes
Time may tick and life gets shorter
Sitting here in this chair
Wondering what tomorrow will be
Maybe were all wondering the same
It is not just me
You may of heard
"Life is what you make of it"
Yes that is true
Also you have to worry about
The "wrong crowd"
Sometime or another in life
You think life could not get any better
Or there may be a time
When you think
There is nothing out there
It is only you who can make a change
Move on into this world
This life and discover the new
Time will eventually give you something
That you thought you could never have or find
Myself is yet so young
But has moved on as well
Happiness and love
Has grown around me
Enjoy
Live and Discover the good.

Stormy Days

Sitting in silence
Soft music surrounds
While everything is calm
At this moment
Mind running with thoughts
Confusion and heartbreak
Why why why?
Then getting up running about
Cleaning until the next break.
Kids running loose
Dogs tearing up the place
And Jerry Springer is on
I'm too young for this I say
Cannot enjoy life
Not this way.

Hearing Them

Voices, voices around me
Voices I cannot stop that surrounds me
Millions of them and only I can hear
Is that so only me to hear those voices
Spoken in different languages by different people
High pitch low pitch they are now combining
Listen…can you hear the voices
The mumbling and blabbing of all those voices
Why won't they go away to even stop
Can you hear them I can
Hearing all those voices.

That Memorial Weekend

Waking up thought it was going to be the best day had it all planned
Until the incident with the four-wheeler going straight forwards
Changing the gears what happened I just lost control
Went right over the bank remembering the fall
Crashing into the creek below
It was a scary feeling knowing that my face
Was going to hit like a slap against the wall
Then as I slowly lifted my head I hear the motor disappear
Water running down my pale, cold face
From a distance you could hear them calling "are you o.k."
I'm trying to climb the bank to let them know but I can't
I have to lie down for I am too weak and it hurts so I just wait
Inspecting me from head to toe they notice something beneath my clothes
As they pulled my pant leg up I looked down and wished I hadn't
Because I seen a big hole
This made me shake even more
So for now I was worried that maybe it was too deep
As the kids around looked about they kindly helped out
Then a sweet gentleman carries me upon that hill into the house
Still in pain but not much because I was in shock
What is taking so long I ask but you cannot rush a guy like that
For he has his own pace
Finally getting to the Galax hospital they take me in
And oh boy how they doctored me up I was in so much pain
I could not wait till the final end
A four-wheeler can be so much fun but can cause scars
All this time I did have a special someone by my side
Encouraging me that I can do this
He told me that it hurt him to see me upon that bed
For I do care for him he is a gift to all and to me
I am so lucky the wreck was very respectable
As he says very respectable.

Gone

Some things are not meant to be in life
Even though we often say
It will last it is going to last forever
Seeing it now it is all in the past
There was once a love
That was sure enough to be true
But now growing up it grows apart from you
The blaming starts the lies grow
Then there is no more of that love
What we had was once sure enough to be true.

Greatest Feeling

Wanting to scream out
To let my feeling run free within
So alive and with passionate that I cannot keep inside
What a great experience a rush that goes beyond
Rushing everywhere within me
It makes me feel so blind and happily feeling great
With smiles that glow you can see a mile away
Wake up world there is so much
And I have found what I have desired
A part of what is truly making my heart and me so bright
For he is so gentle and understanding
The man I long to love.

That Night

Thoughts running
Through the head
The wind picking up
More and more
Having no one to blame
But wanted to
Cannot except it
The wrong that has become
Kept feeling
Worse and worse
A person questioning
What is the matter
Wanting to only escape
For this no it was not the way
Feeling so aggravated and afraid
More thoughts running
Through the head
Did not want to think about that
No it was too awful
That somehow can go away
A little blue right now
It will all pass by real soon
Maybe in the mind
Crying even harder
Than before telling the self
To cheer up
There is another tomorrow.

Have to Go On

We said we would love each other
And really meant it
Cared for one another
Like no other
Then we started to grow apart
Because something was just not right
Started keeping the secrets
And did not want to speak
One night as I came home
Remembering it so clearly
Talked to the neighbor
And he told me sad news
Which I did not want to hear
Total shock for my love
The one I was suppose to wed
Had broken in
Broken in their home
Not once but twice
Why did he do that
For I would like to know
But he could not tell me
And so I could not handle it
He had to go
Maybe that was the only way
That showed he was not the one for me
For things do come in mysterious ways
Living by myself
Yes things are different
But I admit I like it so
What was in the past
Will always last in the memories
To never forget
To look upon those years that we had
Even though they were just a couple.

Come On You're Adults

Fussing and fighting
All the time
Please you two
Your acting like little children
Even though
You have some of your own
You still carry on
While their standing by your side
They hear your little cries
Why do you do
The things you do
Knowing a bit of too much information
About on another maybe true
Or maybe trying to over power the other
But come on blow it off you two
You have to live your life
And I try to help out
But I always get stuck in the middle
While one is saying this and that
You're hurting others and yourselves
Come on now
You are adults so act it.

First Things

Being here at work
He would come in and do his job
Of course he would catch up
On a few rumors on the side
Did not pay much attention to him at first
Him coming through the gate to take out the trucks
Did not know he was watching me with those loving eyes
He finally asked if I would like to go out
It was late so we went to the Waffle House
Then it was days and weeks
After that I would not speak
He began to wonder
Well he knew that I was taken
I was just afraid that it might lead
Into something else so I backed away
All of a sudden
Things began to change as we became friends
I realized about my present relationship
Which was not the best
I've always wanted to have things
To explore so I gave it a try
Which now it has been almost a year
And Newgie has given me many smiles
Since then his name is well known among the guards
And he has been really trying
To concentrate on putting his head on straight
Which I am no help for when were around together
He likes to stay up late
He is like a sweet bird
Not wanting to touch bottom so he lets out his wings
Wrapping them around me
So we can fly both flying slowly in the sky.

Concerned for Her

Who was that, that girl
Looking so sweet but yet she seems
Like a remorse of some kind
To render in the thoughts
Of being something else, could it be
The guilt across her face
That you could only see
Her hopes was there
Within deep inside
Which she only needed to bring out
For the longest time
She has kept a burden
Many burdens inside and will not tell
For what she hides she seems to be kind.
Some days she takes
Real good care of herself and looks fine
While others she goes about
Having nothing to fear
Although she keeps it
Well hidden inside for no one to see.
A brave soul she is
For she hardly ever lets the ones around know anything
But some knows her
They can plainly see she is dying inside.

VIII

She Went Away

Many years went by
The coldness grew
She was fading away
All is left now is the precious memories.

There

I was there and you were there
But out there, it was nowhere.
Wait, now we are here and no there
We are alone nowhere to go.
Faced upon the darkness growing
Hearing only a whisper
"We are alone out there".

Winter

Summer was maybe here
Fall has blown away
Now comes the time
When winter is coming near
The soft green leaves
Are disappearing
Falling heavily on the ground
Turning into crispy brown
Winter is near
The snow may come any day now
The night skies
Are getting clear
For you can see
The bright stars above
While the white moon is shining
Making the dark become light
The brisk cool smell
Is in the air
Because winter
Is yet soon to be here.

Golden Moon

Clear of darkness
Winds of no part
Viewing the sky
Settle ness
Of the golden moon a rising
A meaning of boldness
Beauty beyond
How to tell
Staring
The distance was near.

Years Of Alone

Thinking of the man of loneliness
A house of many rooms
All empty no one to speak to
If he calls out it is nothing
Years and years
Soaking into what he thinks is normal
Not going over was he invited
Hidden into a shell
Is there a passion
A want to go out
Is there a use
These walls hang memories
For never taken down
A sad face seen
Always there into a frown
Opened to nothing.

Picture

It is as simple
As a picture
Hanging on a wall
It is as easy
As watching the sun
Disappear upon those trees.

A child growing
So fast
That you did not
Get all those moments
Those steps.

Thinking life
Is it hard
As an candy cane
But not as sweet.

Seeing elders
Shrink like
Dried raisins
Tears falling
Like a summer rain.

Life
Is it as simple.

Sail Tonight

Heading out into the deep
Of the bluest seas
The wind picks up sail
Knots going higher
Sunsets lower
The sprays of the salted water
Landing on the face
A course planned
To camp once there
Yet peace taken over
The rocking
Shining of the moon
Waters blackened
No blue tonight
Morning peers
Sunrise upon waters
Golden circle appears
Shining onto me
Clear skies
Freshness near
After a sail of a night.

Mexico Market

Standing
Looking at all the goods
Rows and aisles
Of mountainous junk
From fake jewels
To statues
And Mexican hats
Every stand
Of every corner
Mexicans say
You will love this
How about this one
Buy this to wear
It is a junkies paradise
All at your hands
Treasures of all kinds
Tables
Looking the same
Turn this way
Again the same
Still yet
They make a sell.

Invested Home

Building into something
That has taken time
Years of thinking
Praying and saving
Wondering if its the right thing
Full of devotion
A project worth building
An investment there after
Patience yet stressful
Choices of picks
Decisions on sorts
Many of buying
Money of the unknown
The final end
A dream home.

No Fit

Living in this place
How do I do it
The question keeps popping
This home of un-rules
A playhouse
Just space being used
Why I wonder
I stay I stay
Can I go anywhere
Pay more to enjoy
Saving money
Yes I am
But why
Do I like this place
Un-organized
Un-designed
Why.

Only Yourself

A girl of no dreams
Wondering on this planet
With children of her own
But as a child herself
With no searching of hopes
She sees families
And wants to be like them
She wants to act
To do the way
They live their life
I have wondered
Even asked her
When are you going
To start living your own life
Why pretend can't you just be you
Live your own life
Be your own self
Start dreaming
Set goals and succeed
In being you.

To Him

Listening to the sweet voice
That speaks so clear of only horror
Of what has become of him
My heart wanted to reach out to him
To give him no more pain.
As he speaks the truth
That I never dreamed of
Such images started to float
Into my mind my thoughts
My poor love
What a terrible
Dramatic experience you went through
To discover that in your life
And will never forget the moment.

For he was a victim
Waiting at the line of all he had left
Which he thought was the end
We may ask why the good people seem to have much pain
Some are thankful enough to go on each day
If I could only free the sorrow the pain
He holds inside I would
For he says he does have much to thank
For he is alive today walking and talking
So he goes on each day and prays.

To Cry Alone

Many people
Would rather
Share the happiness
That you throw out
Than to sympathize
With all the sorrow
Pain that you have
Why
Because it is
Much easier
That a way
Usually they
Have enough
On their own mind
It is like laugh and the world
Will laugh with you
Cry and you cry
Alone.

To Make It Count

I hear your voice
On the other end
My heart is aching
Longing to be by your side
To be near
To hold you so close
For I am here for you
And I believe we both need
The chance to go on
To make everyday count
To show that we do love each other
That we do really care
For I am opened
Only for you do I make it count.

The Changes

Time changes
Because I once
Said that you
Were mine
All mine
Now you have
Slammed the door
Walked right out
Out of my door
Without saying goodbye
Time changes
We were once in love
Nothing could of
Come between us
But look now
No sweet baby
You are just a someone
That came and gone
You're a behind
There is a no more.

To Not Frown

Do not be around
The ones that
Do make you frown
Making you do those things
That you know
You should not
Or maybe
Calling you bad names
Do not be
Around that wrong
Hanging out
Thinking you
Too cool
No that is not
The way
Things like that
Only make you
Frown.

No Change

You do not
Have to change
For I love you
Being with you
What you are is very special
You are you
To me that means so much
That is coming from my heart
The first time that we met
I thought
Now I like it
For it grows
Do not change
I love you for who you are.

Ruin

Can another person
Ruin the life
Of another
For the future
For only
That one person
Listening
Could over the years
Be destroyed
Cause of telling
Saying this
Doing that
To go no where
That person
Is just one
Could they
Ruin another life
Destroying.

In Much

It was a cool night
In March
Both looking out
Seeing the moon
Reflection upon
The water
Sitting upon
The huge rock
Side by side
Feeling the warmth
Touches of the skin
He softly kissing
Warmness on the neck
Goose bumps appear
Not moving anywhere
Wanting to only
Enjoy this moment
So calm
So peaceful
They came back
To this place
Another night
To enjoy
Once again.

Over Me

Are you over me
For are you
Over me now
No phone calls
You never make
No coming over
No any mores
Is your mind clear
Clear of my face
Is there another
If there is
I hope they treat you right
With do respect
I am proud of you
For going on
I know that it was hard
At first
But you did it
I knew you could
I will always
Be there for you
A friend.

Country Boy

He is from
The country
Were he works
On the fields
And like to hear
The gossip everyday
Getting up
In time to see
The noon
Gets in a days work
Just before two
He is all country
We know he cannot
Never will be
That person to change
For being just him
Is his way
That is the truth.

There Will Be

It is not to long now
The burning sun will go down
Down behind those mountains
Only a few more minutes
The dark will appear
Sinking
Sinking
The sun is going
The dark will now come
Waiting
Waiting
For the tomorrow
To see the sun
Once more.

Rule vs. Limits

There are rules
There are limits
What is the difference
Thought they
Were the same
A rule is the rule
Which we go by
And stick with it
Then there are limits
You push to the limit
What we understand
To be right
Makes sense to us
Although
We know the limit
We sometimes
Go beyond
We stick to the rule.

Reaching Up

The little boy
Is now seven
Growing up
Learning as much
Exploring what is around
For he soon
Will become a man
No father to guide him
To show him
The boy stuff
Like hunting
Fishing
Football
No
For he left
To never see again
A mother being there
Supporting and caring
Giving all she can
Struggling through life
Cause times are hard
She wants him to be
Strong
To live
To laugh
And to enjoy
What lays ahead.

All This

No money to spend
No food to get
You'd think it
Was a waste to live
Worrying
When you shouldn't
Wishing that the next day
Will be different
Than this day
Doesn't even matter
To see Friday
But all this complaining
What does it do
Nothing
So I'll just shut up
Sit here and think
Of another
Maybe about
Something special.

College

Only a couple days now
And the day will come
When I go and enter
The doors to the future
I hear it's not too bad
But others say
It could be
Very, very sad
A little worried
Because I'm wanting
To do the best
But in the years
I know it will suit me
Just fine
And I can go on
With my life
But then
What is next after that?
There is so much
And so many things
I want to do
My mind stays full
I sometimes cannot think
So the only thing I can do now
Is just finish school and see what later
Later of what I'll do
Or maybe even go
A totally different way.

Hanger

Coming to this place
I call it the barn
Or more like the farm
Because it is
Right in the middle
Of a cow field
Doing some work around
He finally got
The concrete poured
As I'm cleaning inside
He wants me to help him pull the stakes
Out of the ground
Got to use the tractor
It was different
Now he is leveling
The dirt with it
As I just take a break
Watching from the side
Sitting in the Jeep
He is trying to finish
The airplane hanger
Not too much for me to do
So I'll just stay right here
On the side and wait.

My Fault

Got some
Hot Shot
Wanted to clear
Some bees away
I seen a grasshopper
Cross my path
And thought
I'd give it a try
Sprayed the grasshopper
At least twice
He started jumping around
So I sprayed it again
And then
Oh it was so sad
The poor little thing
Began to just lie
Gasping for I know the air
The little thing curled up
Jerking wanting the pain
To just go away
There was nothing
I could do
It was my entire fault
There he lies dying
The poor little thing
It is my entire fault.

Look Deep Within

There has to be more out there
Then just dying
Working
And having babies
As I have been told
Yes there is more out there
In this world
Which we look at it
In a different point
Helping out
Around us today
We can surely make a change
Putting smiles on faces
So we can see
The little sparkles
Glowing in their eyes
Looking up to see
Our Lord
To give many thanks
To Him we are not
All here to just do
The little things
But so much more
There is a whole lot
Out there
It is you
Who has to make it
Worth going forward
We have to look
Deep within
To make a change.

Ocean

You want to go back
To see it again
To feel that feeling
Beneath your toes
To run upon and leap out
To fall to swim out
Like a fish
Tasting the salt
So beautiful to see
The clearness it gives
And the smell
Oh so sweet and fresh
The ocean
Hearing it slap
Against the stone wall
So you want to go back
And get a taste of it all
Well o.k.
Maybe
The following weekend
If you're up to it
That would be so nice
And exciting
After all, it isn't everyday
That you get to experience
Any of that around here
In the hills
So will relax
Get a taste of it
In the fall.

Corn Worm

I help pick the corn
To bring in an eat
I cut and plucked
At least eight
Got it washed up
And in the pot to boil
As I was talking
There something was
Right on my shirt
Who knows what it was
Fuzzy and green
With many legs
I felt it as it had a sting
I screamed and kicked
Finally Ma shoved it off
My skin red
Had a hurt feeling to it
And it looked
Like bubbles appearing
I'm never going
Corn picking again
I don't want
To meet the green worm again.

A Little Girl

Long ago
It seems
Like ages ago
A little girl
Set all alone
Sitting in
Her little corner
She had a habit
Still does
Always biting
On her finger nails
But that little girl
Was just alone
No one to come by
To tell her the tales
Years go by
She is a young lady
Not so much alone
For she
Having made
Many friends
And would like
To keep it that way
But yet still
Inside she feels
As if she is
Still that little girl
All alone.

Clouds

Floating
Drifting
Slowly above my head
They seem to pacify me
As I lay my eyes on them
When the sun starts to set
They reflect with many colors
Like looking out into another world
So peacefully
So heavenly
They are the clouds.

What Should

One, two
What shall I do
Three, four
Should I stop deciding
On which door to open
Or go on with five
Which for right now
It may be undecided
What shall I do
Chances are I might end up
In circles with no clue
At the same starting point
Oh my, one, two
What shall I do.

Busy Time

When holidays come around
They can easily be such a pain
Taking on extra hours
Just to catch up
But the money is going down the drain
Having only a little time
To get your shopping done
Hurrying up here and there
Keeping your balance trying to stand
When the holidays come a rollin around
There goes most of the plans
You're hustling here and here
And there and there.

Matter of Time

The sleet comes down
And only in a matter of minutes
The roads began to ice
The hearing of it hit
Hitting the ground
The moon gives it a shine
As it sticks to the limbs
Like glass that can easily break
Break only in time
The ice smelling so fresh
Filling your lungs with clean air
Watching it come down
Coming down
In only a matter of time.

U.A.W Party

Music had its
People having fun
Drinking this and that
As we and some others
Getting on the dance floor
Trying not to have the same pace
But just to have a little taste
To jiggling butts
To on the floor
We wanted to carry on
Got only two dances out of Lori
Rubbing her body all over me
Then instantly she was gone
Flat on the table
Just a drooling.

To Get Away

Feels as if my mind
Is at its last remaining
Feels as if I cannot
Take any more within my mind
My mind feels as if it is taking in
Many things that seem to not make sense
Day after day, feels as if everything is the same
Day after day my mind cannot take much more
I'm going insane
Doesn't anybody see that
I really need to spend time with just me
To relax and to just get to get away.

Mystery Man

Like a Fantasy world
That I live in
Every since I met you
I know the reality
Will never come
But somehow all I do
Is keep thinking about you
A picture that I keep
Tucked away in a secret place
I gradually look upon it
And a piece of me is lost
Wanting to touch your face
To hear the sound of your voice
You've changed me inside
And a part of me wants to cry
Wanting to reach out a hand
To grasp
To only hold you
Once again.

By Your Side

You don't have to say a word
I can see it in your eyes
I know you're not playing any games
You just like to take your time
As long as it takes
I will be right here by your side
Just waiting, waiting to hear
To hear those sweet, sweet words
Coming straight out of you from your heart
I will
I will be right by your side.

The Distance

How far will you go
How high would you touch
To reach to travel many miles
To go beyond what thoughts are to have
To hold
To only go forth
What is the circumstance
What is the plan
Is this reachable
Is it determined
Tell me
Tell me
For how is it
How far will you go.

Beauty Found

To find
To grab
Beauty
The painting of beauty
Wondering how it was made
Images that have never been seen
Lifting
Taking control of your mind
For the power of it is real
Too real
The beauty grasps taking your breath away
The feeling of the holding on
For you want it but there is no touch
Only seeing
Seeing the beauty.

World of Fear

Living in a world of fear
For every turn that one person makes
Leads into a disappointment
For every truth that is spoken
Leads into hate
Only wanting to live that simple life
But asking thyself what is simple
Working every day to pay the bills
But while doing so you're unsure
About the secured ness of your job
Everybody is trying to get back at one another
No person is as good
For that one is always better
In the eyes seeing their loneliness
They suffer
Wanting to get only attention
But only receives hate
A world of confusion
A place that has its only name
The pain increases
The vultures feast
Going every day
Thinking their highly
But they are no different than the rest.

Steps Back

One so young
And both so fragile
Seeing the sadness
Feeling the coldness
As both fear for the future
Wondering if the moments will last
Tears filling the eyes
For the thoughts always haunting
The mind racing ahead
Not realizing the present is still here
The aching of the heart spreading
But somewhere a piece is wanting to love
To give that love
Searching for the right one
Finding it
Then looking at the problems that could occur
Wanting to go that step
But the heart holds back not wanting to get hurt
Protecting, holding, so afraid.

Praying Words

Thank you Jesus for this day
Help Momma in every way
Bless us all
Take out the sins
And give us the good within
Heal the broken
Take away their pain
Thank you Jesus
Amen.

Open Heart

Empty your thoughts
Look at me
And please see that I am here
Here with you
Do not let the future haunt you so
Hold my hand my love
Remember that faith is the key
It is hard to not be afraid and confused
But open
Open your heart to me.

Switched

It was a clear blue sky
Sun shining so bright
Birds chirping
Children playing
Looking towards the huge mountains
The clouds started to form
Getting black
Lightning then flashing
Thunder shouting
Rain pouring onto the ground
Sun hides
Birds fly
The children runs inside.

Catch The Rain

Are you chasing the rain
Drops fall
Your arms are wide out
To catch the falling rain
Nothing to grab onto
Nothing to feel
Spilling down drops at a time
And you are trying to catch them all
Pouring now
Running down faster
Getting wet may get sick
But you stand there
Trying to catch the falling rain
No feelings it has no love
No regrets
All alone
You are trying to hold on
To something you cannot catch
And your chasing the fallen rain.

Cannot Help

He cannot help but to want to know her
Seeing her beauty not only out but what's within
He cannot help wanting to love her
For all is too much
Seeking into these green-green eyes
Thinking that independence was the only way
Until she swept him away
Liking that smile
Liking the surrounds wasn't in no hurry
For there is everyday
To go finding that feelings
That came unnoticed
Finding that gal
That was so young and right
Cannot help but wanting to hold her so near
So many times cannot help.

Let me show you

How my love
Can build a tower
A tower so high
That the sky
Will kiss it
And you will adore it.

Time Stood Still

Is was that one winter
Driving through
Running along side of the chilly river
Climbing upon a rock
Now looking down seeing the river
Looking back as the moon gives its kiss
Holding me so close
But barely knowing each other
We sat there that night as time passed.

Wrong

What is it now
You pack my make up
For you say this is grounding
Then you take my blow dryer
The iron curler
I say what did I do
What did I do
The only thing I can figure out
Is that it's your moods
One day you're fine
The next is fallen down
This house is a wreck
It's not my fault or their fault
I'm not to blame
So why are you taking my things.

Junk In Front

As I sit here there
Seeing in front
The table what I think is junk
Realizing this junk
Was just a clipboard that's used
Over there is a book for me
To read to further educate
A lock, ticks – hearing and seeing the time
Which I am thankful to have
Over there sits a telephone
Discovered and used everyday
On the left is a radio
Many channels it plays
Listening to songs that
Some will make you laugh, dance, or cry
Then there is my soda
A nice refreshing drink
With popcorn on the side – crunch
Sitting here I thought
All this was just junk
But its some things
I should be thankful for
For we need this junk.

Oh God

I am writing to you today
To tell and pray
About all those little things
Sitting here I look to you for the answers
I lift my hand up
And ask you Lord so many things
Yes God
I am writing to you today
All my thoughts
And my prayers
I am looking up to you
My Lord for the answers.

Tree Stands Tall

How is that tree standing
So tall
No raindrops
No moisture
Just the dryness yet it stands there alone
As you ponder you come upon
A moment of silence between you
And mother nature
Just standing there
Tasting
Sucking in what all she gives
Yet you still think
How is that tree so tall without any rain at all.

My Life Behind

Life how did it start out
Was this the moment to tell
A little girl waiting wanting to be elsewhere
A dream that has no ending
Time that felt like forever a life of something
To be where just anywhere
Starting out it could take hours
Many pages to flip problems experienced to tell
Possibly I could sit down and spill
Hardships, aches, and bruises
Living to live but wanting to die to escape
People they go through so much but why a little child
Could they just bloom into something beautiful
Be somebody have a family
Grow up into love and have dreams
Seeing sunshine to be happy of what is there
Not to be sad wishing God would take them
Curled up away a world so big but living so small
A knowing of nothing no parents to guide or support
There was nothing saying should life go on
Do you want to hear more
To tell this brings haunting memories

Leather straps, boards, and slaps
These problems who wants to here them right
A story of our lives growing to see
Getting out of the wretched
Then there is the thinking
Of course that will always be
The dreams the doings the never endings
Asking why lessons to be learned
Living like that to grow realizing what is to be
Are we to know right and wrong
To face tomorrow making the decisions
Saying I will make it better so much but how in words
Being alone that little girl
Writing in her diary for that is all she had
No one to understand crying all those years
Wishing and then praying
Looking back it brings tears
Horrible days of misery
My life how it went and how it goes on
Grown into a change a woman going forward
Still here living and smiling for it does get better
My life how does it start out
I can tell you now that I am grateful
Happier inside a someone that has flown
And thanking God because he did care.